Bow Down:
The Heart of A True
Worshipper

A 30-Day Devotional
Based on writings of David

by Heather Adams

Contents

Introduction

David is famous for being called "a man after God's own heart" (Acts 13:22), and rightly so. In his words and actions he modeled what it means to worship with your whole being. And as he sang, played his harp, wrote songs and danced, David invited the Israelites to join him in having a deeper, more joyful relationship with their God.

Like many people, I used to equate worship mainly with music. But in studying David's life and writing, I've gained a broader vision of what worship is meant to be. God, as usual, has greater things in store for us than we can come up with ourselves!

1 Chronicles 16 is an account of David giving instruction regarding worship as the ark was returned to Jerusalem. "That day David first committed to Asaph and his associates this psalm of thanks to the LORD..." Within this 28-verse song, David lays out a comprehensive list of what I call "worship action words." Reading this for the first time left me excited, but wondering if all these activities could really be worship.

The more I studied the psalms David wrote, the more echoes I found of this passage. He referred back to this list again and again, with no hint of doubt that yes, God did see them as worship. And so I started trying out different items on the list, in times of personal and also corporate worship. It didn't take long before I noticed an increase in awareness of God's presence in my life, and a sense of gratitude and praise for Him.

That is why I decided to use 1 Chronicles 16 as a basis of this devotional book. I have chosen 15 elements mentioned in this passage to explore. Then, I've found verses that David wrote in Psalms to highlight each one - the "echoes", so to speak. For each element I've written two devotionals, the first puts the focus on David, and the second includes my own personal insights and thoughts.

Included with each study is one of two exercises:

- A *Prayer Starter* - Prayer is not only a way to worship, but a tool for growing in understanding of God. Often after studying scripture, I find myself turning right to prayer, sharing my questions or insights with God. When I give Him that time, I end up with greater clarity and I feel more equipped with the wisdom I need to live each day for Him.

- An *Action Point* - We are meant to be active participants in our faith. God wants us to partner with Him as He grows us into strong men and women of faith. As I learn new truths and ideas, I need to apply them to my life so that they really take root. Then I can help others see more of God in their lives, too.

My hope is that by learning more about David and his vision of worship, your own walk will be enriched. Let the Holy Spirit guide you as you read, write a prayer or work on an action point. Then, be ready to go on a great adventure with God as you start to experience worship in a bigger way!

Heather Adams

1 Chronicles 16:7-36

That day David first committed to Asaph and his associates this psalm of thanks to the LORD: Give thanks to the LORD, call on his name; make known among the nations what he has done. Sing to him, sing praise to him; tell of all his wonderful acts. Glory in his holy name; let the hearts of those who seek the LORD rejoice. Look to the LORD and his strength; seek his face always. Remember the wonders he has done, his miracles, and the judgments he pronounced, O descendants of Israel his servant, O sons of Jacob, his chosen ones. He is the LORD our God; his judgments are in all the earth. He remembers his covenant forever, the word he commanded, for a thousand generations, the covenant he made with Abraham, the oath he swore to Isaac. He confirmed it to Jacob as a decree, to Israel as an everlasting covenant: "To you I will give the land of Canaan as the portion you will inherit." When they were but few in number, few indeed, and strangers in it, they wandered from nation to nation, from one kingdom to another. He allowed no man to oppress them; for their sake he rebuked kings: "Do not touch my anointed ones; do my prophets no harm." Sing to the LORD, all the earth; proclaim his salvation day after day. Declare his glory among the nations, his marvelous deeds among all peoples. For great is the LORD and most worthy of praise; he is to be feared above all gods. For all the gods of the nations are idols, but the LORD made the heavens. Splendor and majesty are before him; strength and joy in his dwelling place. Ascribe to the LORD, O families of nations, ascribe to the LORD glory and strength, ascribe to the LORD the glory due his name.Bring an offering and come before him; worship the LORD in the splendor of his holiness.Tremble before him, all the earth! For great is the LORD and most worthy of praise; he is to be feared above all gods. For all the gods of the nations are idols, but the LORD made the heavens. Splendor and majesty are before him; strength and joy in his dwelling place. Give thanks to the LORD, for he is good; his love endures forever. Cry out, "Save us, O God our Savior; gather us and deliver us from the nations, that we may give thanks to your holy name, that we may glory in your praise." Praise be to the LORD, the God of Israel, from everlasting to everlasting. Then all the people said "Amen" and "Praise the LORD."

Day 1
Give Thanks

"I will give you thanks in the great assembly; among throngs of people I will praise you."

Psalm 35:18

As a king, David had great influence, and used it to encourage outward displays of worship in his nation. He himself set the example: he shouted out his confidence in God in front of two armies while facing Goliath (1 Samuel 17); he danced in the procession as the ark came into Jerusalem (2 Samuel 6); he wrote songs full of praise, psalms that were regularly used in the temple.

Clearly he was excited about giving thanks to his God. More than a daily ritual, it was as a vital part of his being. He knew without a connection to God, his life would have little meaning. The awareness of his own needs and of a God who could meet every one brought him great joy, a delight he couldn't help but express.

God has always wanted to be close to His people, and to bless them. And the king whose heart beat for God must have felt grief for those who didn't understand the kind of relationship they could enjoy with their Heavenly Father. Beyond knowing laws and basic principles, God commanded His people to celebrate *Him*. David led the way, his gratitude bubbling over into singing, laughing and even dancing before His Lord!

Prayer Starter:
God is your Jehovah Jireh, your Provider. Write a prayer thanking Him for the blessings He gives you each day, and include some recent examples.

_____

_____

_____

_____

_____

_____

Day 2
Give Thanks

"You turned my wailing into dancing; you removed my sackcloth and clothed me with joy, that my heart may sing to you and not be silent. O LORD my God, I will give you thanks forever."

Psalm 30:11-12

There's something about thanking God that changes our heart's direction. In the middle of a difficult day, for instance, I can open my mouth to vent, or to say something more positive. It's up to me which one comes out.

Showing God appreciation 'lifts my countenance'. Thanking Him takes me from a self-centered to a God-centered focus. Once I'm thinking more of Him than me, my mood improves. Is it always easy to maintain an attitude of gratitude? No! But there are a couple of habits that keep me spending more time glorifying than grumbling:

1. I *choose* to be grateful.
Simple maybe, but making the decision to thank God every day makes a big impact on my mindset. I try to start each day by lifting up His works and His character.

2. I look beyond the present moment.
During challenging times, looking around me or remembering past blessings jumpstarts my thanks-giving. Whether in scripture or just outside my window, I never have to look far to see a miracle.

Action Point:

The next time you find yourself grumbling or upset, try to stop and think of one thing to give thanks to God for. It can be as simple as the beauty of the day, or the money to pay a bill. It doesn't matter what you choose, as much as deciding to change your focus for a moment. Give your thanks aloud - hearing your own voice can actually train your mind. Once you name one thing, chances are more will spring to mind. Write each thing down, as a kind of gratitude journal:

_____

_____

_____

_____

_____

_____

Day 3
Sing to Him

"I will praise you, O LORD, with all my heart; before the "gods" I will sing your praise."

Psalm 138:1

I sometimes wish we had recordings of the music David wrote. Scripture has many mentions of David singing to the Lord, such as in 2 Samuel 22, an act that was probably as natural to him as breathing. The psalms David wrote to sing were full of prayer and praise, each showing a deep love for God.

David could have been content to express his own worship and hope others followed his example. But he considered music to be a vital part of his nation's religious life, and a way to strengthen faith. So, along with his songwriting, he founded an ambitious music ministry at the temple - at one time thousands of singers and musicians helped to lead during a single service!

Singing about the truths of God and His works is an effective way to remember and celebrate them. David, having spent so many years praying and praising, from the hillside to the throne, knew the power of music. He wanted to teach his people and ignite a passion for God within them. And the music he made to do that must have been wonderful!

Prayer Starter:
God doesn't care about how perfect your singing voice is - He is after your heart. Write a prayer about your willingness to life up your voice to Him in song:

_____

_____

_____

_____

_____

Day 4
Sing to Him

"Sing to the LORD, you saints of his; praise his holy name."
Psalm 30:4

Music was an integral part of Israel's worship life. Songs were written to lift up prayers, as well as to remind the people of God's works and teach about His character.

Today churches still incorporate music into their services. Unfortunately, differences of opinion over which type of music to use have sometimes led to division within congregations. As a result, people can end up distracted or frustrated. How many have missed out on the life-changing potential of a service because they didn't like the song selection?

Having an "us or them" mindset is destructive. And there's another way. If we can look beyond categories - labeling a song as 'just a hymn' or 'just a chorus' - and favoring our own preferences, we might see the power of many kinds of music to:

• Invite the congregation into worship
• **Nurture** unity among members
• **Share** new ideas
• Prepare the hearts of attenders
• Increase the depth of the sermon teaching
• Remind everyone of basic Christian truths
• Encourage and uplift people

Action Point:

Do you have a preference of worship song styles? What about it do you like? Try listening to some other styles that are less familiar to you. Can you find something to appreciate, such as powerful lyrics or an emotion it evokes? Write some of your observations:

_____

_____

_____

_____

_____

_____

Day 5
Tell

"Many, O LORD my God, are the wonders you have done. The things you planned for us no one can recount to you; were I to speak and tell of them, they would be too many to declare."

Psalm 40:5

David certainly had the gift of evangelism. His psalms reveal an urgent need to let everyone know as much as possible about God. David simply couldn't help himself! And Psalm 40 is a great example of how telling a personal experience can become an invitation to others.

In verse 5 David wrote that he could never recount the amazing things God has done - there would be too many to tell. But he has already started out the psalm by sharing a praise item. Verse 2 talks about being delivered out of trouble to a better place. And the next passage reflects a renewed spirit of worship in response to God's blessings. Gratitude pours out of his words.

David didn't share these kinds of experiences to boast or to set himself above anyone else. He knew that telling the world about God would keep the fire burning in his own heart. And he wanted others to see the possibilities and hope that exist for anyone who commits to living godly lives.

Prayer Starter:

It's true that we if we recounted everything God has done we'd never finish talking. But have you even *started* telling about Him yet? If not, why not? Write Him a prayer, confessing any fears or doubts you have about speaking out, and asking Him for boldness:

_____

_____

_____

_____

_____

Day 6
Tell

"One generation will commend your works to another; they will tell of your mighty acts."

Psalm 145:4

On Thanksgiving Eve, my church holds a "testimony slam". Anyone who wants to get up and share can participate, choosing one of two themes to focus on: how we came to know and accept Christ as our Savior, or what difference having Jesus as our Lord has made in our lives.

The first time I went I was a little unsure what to expect. I figured it would be a nice gathering, and a chance to hear some interesting stories. But what I didn't plan on was how powerful the experience would be for all of us. Listening to other people tell of God's work in their lives effected me in a couple of special ways:

1. I was reminded that I belong to a family.
As humans, we can tend toward an independent "me-centered" mindset. Spending time with our brothers and sisters and sharing tales of God's goodness brings comfort and encouragement we won't get on our own.
2. I saw that we all had a common story.
Our circumstances, experiences and even generations might be different, but we all have the same basic need to be fully known and fully loved. No matter who we are, all of us must go to the same source to get those needs met.

Action Point:

Take time to write a short testimony, using one of the two ideas already mentioned:

- How you came to know and accept Christ as your Savior
OR
- What difference having Jesus as your Lord has made in your life.

Be as specific as possible, remembering details and emotions you had. Share your testimony with someone else and invite them to try writing their own.

_____

_____

_____

_____

_____

_____

Day 7
Glory In His Name

"Glory in his holy name; let the hearts of those who seek the LORD rejoice."

Psalm 105:3

The word 'glory' is often used as a noun in the Bible - "the glory of the Lord," for example. But here, David uses it as a verb, even a command to his readers. Was he just being poetic, or using it instead of other verbs simply to add variety? Maybe, but a search of the word in the Merriam Webster Dictionary resulted in a couple of interesting definitions that catch some of David's heart for God:

To exult with triumph

David's worship of God is filled with not just praises, but reasons for that praise. He often recounts episodes of God's rescue or provision in the past. And being so aware of those times reminds David that his Lord is already victorious. So he worships with confidence in God's might and deep love for him - His God is over all!

To rejoice proudly

When he talks about God, David shows a sense of humility about himself but a full-blown pride in his God. He delights in sharing examples of God's character and wonders, sounding a bit like a little boy boasting about his father. And David is too excited to stay quiet, vowing "I will praise you, Lord, among the nations..." (Psalm 18:49).

Prayer Starter:

To glory in God's Name means to celebrate all that He is. Write a prayer to the Lord, sharing the emotions that come up in your heart when you meditate on some aspect of His character, such as His strength or faithfulness.

_____

_____

_____

_____

_____

_____

Day 8
Glory In His Name

"I love the house where you live, O LORD, the place where your glory dwells."

Psalm 26:8

I've become very grateful to the custodians at my church, a couple who live nearby. Every Saturday morning, she vacuums and scrubs the bathrooms. He dusts and empties the trash. When they are thanked, they shrug it off, saying "it's our job".

I used to take our building, and them, for granted. But more and more I've come to see our church as a place God has generously given us to gather and to glory in Him. And this couple, I realized, was doing more than just a "job." What might look like simple chores in their hands became worship. They gave their time and abilities in service to God in a practical, tangible way. The work they do enables the rest of us to concentrate more on our Lord while we're there.

Now, we all have the chance to be "custodians for God's house." Under the new covenant through Jesus, we are "temples of the Holy Spirit." Caring for our bodies and minds to make a fit home for God is part of every believer's job. And staying healthy will help prevent distractions to fully worshipping God.

Action Point:

Do you know who takes care of the cleaning duties in your church? If you haven't yet done so, consider volunteering to help, even with a small task. Write down at least 5 things you could offer to do right away. Choose one and then do it!

Extra: God wants to dwell in you! Take an inventory of your overall health. Are there any ways you can start taking better care of yourself to make a good home for Him?

_____

_____

_____

_____

_____

Day 9
Rejoice

"...may the righteous be glad and rejoice before God; may they be happy and joyful."

Certain Christians in every age have seen God as grim, ready to punish for sins. But that view isn't fully accurate. For while God does discipline and even punish at times, scripture often describes a Lord who would much rather celebrate with His people.

Books such as Leviticus list all sorts of occasions to rejoice. Each came in response to something God had done, such as providing a good harvest or victory in battle, and delivering His people out of Egypt. Those times included feasting, gathering of families together, and giving joyful worship to their God.

David understood this heritage of joy that the Israelites had. In many of his psalms we can see him emerge from dark thoughts or feelings to a place of renewed faith. How did he get there? By clinging to the truths he'd learned, and naming wonderful things God had done. Faced with the overwhelming evidence of God's love and goodness, David's reaction was one of joy, and he never hesitated to share his emotion with the nation. I can imagine him laughing out loud, or breaking into song in those moments out of sheer delight. What a wonderful example to set for his kingdom!

Prayer Starter:
Our God is a God of joy! Write a prayer, asking for His help to have a heart to see reasons for rejoicing and to have a desire to join Him in the celebration every day!

_____

_____

_____

_____

_____

Day 10
Rejoice

"Let me hear joy and gladness; let the bones you have crushed rejoice."
Psalm 51:8

My first few years as a Christian were very difficult. I had been struggling for most of my life with depression and anxiety, and brought both right along with me into my new life. Add to that some faulty ideas about God's character, and I was left with little room left for rejoicing. I was too busy pushing and trying to prove myself worthy of God's love.

If I'd understood more then about the Lord I'd accepted, I think I would have experienced a lot more joy each day. In the Old Testament God actually commanded His people to observe times of rejoicing during the year. And we see in the Gospels how Jesus happily joined others in celebrations and parties.

How amazing it was to learn the truth that God already loved me fully, just as I was - I could stop pushing so hard. Then through scripture I caught more and more glimpses of God's "lighter" side. His joy on those pages was overwhelming, and contagious. By allowing myself to express joy, I found healing for past hurts and a hope for what was to come in my life. Now I try to take time every day to stop and imagine God "delighting over me." It lightens my heart and helps me stay glad.

Action Point:

On a scale of one to ten (1 is despairing and 10 is really celebrating), check your "joy level" at a couple of random moments. If your level is low, think about why. Are you focused on problems and concerns and missing the bigger picture of God's plan? Are you forgetting that God has already done great things for you? Read Exodus Chapter 15. Write down some ideas about rejoicing in God's work from the song Moses and Miriam sing, starting in verse 1:

_____

_____

_____

_____

_____

_____

Day 11
Look To The Lord

"Look to the LORD and his strength; seek his face always."
Psalm 105:4

The Message Bible[1] translation of this verse reads, "Keep your eyes open for God; be alert for signs of His presence." And the Strong's Greek Dictionary[2] definition of 'look' is "to see something physical, leading to perception so that a person can take the needed action." In David's case, looking first involved using his eyes and senses to be aware of God and His will, then mindfully making deductions and decisions about how to respond.

This type of looking enriched David's worship life. How? Consider the two main actions in the Message translation:

1. **Keep your eyes open**
David spent his whole life looking toward his Lord, whether for help, comfort, understanding or wisdom. He understood that finding God isn't meant to be a one-time event. God was always doing "a new thing" in and around him, and he didn't want to miss any chance to witness it!

2. **Be alert**
As a shepherd, a king, and a godly man, David had learned the importance of being tuned in, ready to receive what God had for Him. His mindset reflected that truth. It would have been easy to let distractions pull him away, but David was determined to keep his eyes fixed "on things above."

Prayer Starter:
In order to follow God, we have to be watching for Him. Write a prayer asking for help in looking to God first in your life, and to be more aware of how He is working around you:

_____

_____

_____

_____

_____

Day 12
Look To The Lord

"Those who look to him are radiant; their faces are never covered with shame."

Psalm 34:5

At the time I accepted Christ, I was attending a very small fellowship. And within that little family were several wonderful godly women. I remember noticing as I sat among these ladies, "There's something different about them."

I tried, but couldn't quite put my finger on it. They were happier than I was, and more calm, which appealed to me. But it went beyond that. I could almost see a physical difference in their faces, especially as they sang worship songs or spoke about God - a kind of glow.

What makes the face of a believer radiant is spending time close to their Creator. Moses would visit with God in the tent of meeting, and because God's radiance was so bright, he actually had to cover his face for a while afterwards. I believe a version of that can happen today with any one of us.

The more worship we lift up to God, more joy shines through our smiles. As we cast more of our cares upon Him, worry lines start to disappear. As we more fully accept His love and goodness, our eyes reflect deeper compassion for others. I'm so grateful God gave me such good examples as a young Christian. I hope someone has seen at least a spark of that glow in me too.

Action Point:

During your next church service, take a quick peek around the sanctuary. Do you see anyone with that extra "glow" as they worship? Does seeing someone with a "radiant" face inspire you or challenge you? Why? Write some ideas down:

_____

_____

_____

_____

_____

Day 13
Seek His Face

"One thing I ask of the LORD, this is what I seek: that I may dwell in the house of the LORD all the days of my life, to gaze upon the beauty of the LORD and to seek him in his temple."

Psalm 27:4

In Psalm 27 David confidently stated his heart of devotion to God, whom he called his "light and salvation" and his "stronghold." And David used the word 'seek' twice in verse 4, with two different focuses, to give even more expression to his thoughts.

First, he claimed the one thing he wanted from God, namely to stay in His house for the rest of his life. He couldn't actually live in the temple. But he longed to stay "in God's tent" - to seek God's presence in his life. For David had experienced God's faithfulness and deliverance over and over. He he didn't ever want to find himself far from that feeling of shelter and protection.

The next time, 'seek' was used to declare an additional intention of David's heart. It wasn't enough for him to simply live near his Lord. He wanted to engage in an active pursuit of Him - to learn deeper truths and see a greater vision of His beauty. And the claim that ends the psalm, "I will see the goodness of the Lord in the land of the living," resulted from keeping his heart turned to God.

Prayer Starter:

One way David showed his worship to God was by seeking to live near to Him all the time. Write a prayer to the Lord about your desire to stay close to Him, and how that will change the way you live.

_____

_____

_____

_____

_____

_____

Day 14
Seek His Face

"My heart says of you, "Seek his face!" Your face, LORD, I will seek."
                                                                Psalm 27:8

In my early Christian years, I spent a lot of energy striving to have a sense God's presence in my daily life. Insecure in my relationship with Him, what I wanted was evidence that He really loved and cared about me. If I didn't hear from Him right away, I assumed it was my fault. So I'd "pray harder" or try to study longer sections of the Bible, only feeling more separated from Him rather than closer.

I didn't understand then what the Bible meant by "seek." The dictionary definition is "to go in search or quest of." It is the active pursuit of something noble. And when we do this, we'll replace desperate struggle with determined reaching. I was reaching for the noblest thing of all: God's presence in my life, but came up short on my own.

Once I understood the definition of seeking, I had to learn the better approach to it. I needed to realize that my part was to ask humbly for more of God, then to wait patiently and expectantly for Him to reveal Himself to me at the right time - *His* time. How amazing that seeking God was so simple. That truth calmed my mind and gave me the reassurance I needed.

Action Point:

God wants us to put effort toward goals in our lives, most importantly to be more like Him. But we aren't meant to do it on our own.

Write down some practical ways you can seek God by reaching rather than striving.

_____

_____

_____

_____

_____

_____

Day 15
Remember The Wonders

"Remember the wonders he has done, his miracles, and the judgments he pronounced, O descendants of Abraham his servant, O sons of Jacob, his chosen ones.."

Psalm 105:5-6

The nation of Israel had a history of forgetting God. They were especially prone to this when things were going well. It often took a disastrous event to bring them running back to their Lord. David had seen this habit of forgetting, sinning, struggling and crying out to God play out over and over again, and it made him sad. He was determined to do what he could to break that cycle, and knew remembering was an important key.

Psalm 105 is a narrative about God's blessings to His young nation. David starts with a couple verses calling his people to praise. And he gives them the reason in verse 8, saying "He remembers his covenant forever, the word he commanded, for a thousand generations..." Then, through the accounts of Abraham, Isaac, Jacob, Joseph and Moses, David lays out the pattern of God's goodness for His children.

David is hoping that by showing examples of God's memory of His promises, a new cycle will begin among the people: remembering, obeying, blessing, and joyful worship!

Prayer Starter:

How amazing that God never forgets us, His children! Write a prayer, expressing how knowing that makes you feel toward God and your relationship Him.

_____

_____

_____

_____

_____

Day 16
Remember The Wonders

"Praise the LORD, O my soul; all my inmost being, praise his holy name. Praise the LORD, O my soul, and forget not all his benefits..."

Psalm 103:1-2

The act of remembering can be powerful. Memories play out first in our minds, but they usually engage our emotions as well. Recalling events or people can have great value, bringing us deeper understanding of and appreciation of what we've experienced.

I've found that reading Psalm 103 leads me to do some remembering about what God has done, for me and for others. It's easy to skim over those benefits of God and simply be impressed. But when I took the time to slow down and connect with each one, I was overwhelmed!

Let me show you what I mean. The first one, "He forgives all my sins," (v.3) quickly had me doing a mental review. All sorts of sins I'd already committed popped into my mind, along with some guilt and shame. But what God wants me to hold on to isn't the memory of my sin, but how He has always dealt with me in a loving way. It's as if God wants to plant new memories of Him washing me clean of my wrongs. And every time I relive that, my gratitude grows. So does my desire to praise Him!

Action Point:

Look over Psalm 103. Circle each "benefit" as you read it. Then, over the next few days, take time to consider each. Write down any memories that come up from your life. For example: If you ever needed healing, write down your illness or condition. Lift each memory up to God, asking Him to show you how He worked in your life.

Day 17
Declare His Glory

"O Lord, open my lips, and my mouth will declare your praise."
Psalm 51:15

David spent his life declaring the glory of God, even when he faltered. In Psalm 51, David gave a testimony about how God's mercy toward his sinful behavior led him to even deeper worship.

Step 1 - *"Against you, you only, have I sinned and done what is evil in your sight…"* (v.4)
Taking responsibility for the sin - naming and claiming it - showed a humility and submission to God.

Step 2 - *"Cleanse me with hyssop, and I will be clean; wash me, and I will be whiter than snow."* (v. 7)
Asking God for forgiveness showed a desire to walk in His ways.

Step 3 - *"Do not cast me from your presence or take your Holy Spirit from me. Restore to me the joy of your salvation and grant me a willing spirit, to sustain me."* (v.11-12)
Seeking to be reconnected to God showed a heart longing to be close to Him.

Step 4 *"…my tongue will sing of your righteousness. O Lord, open my lips, and my mouth will declare your praise."* (v. 14-15)
Worshipping God in front of others showed a holy boldness to display faith in His goodness.

Prayer Starter:
No matter how we stumble in our faith walk, God's glory continues to shine bright. Write a prayer based on the steps laid out in the devotional, opening up your heart to God, and thanking Him for His mercy and restoration.

_____

_____

_____

_____

_____

Day 18
Declare His Glory

"The heavens declare the glory of God; the skies proclaim the work of his hands."

Psalm 19:1

For many years I didn't think much about the beauty of nature or see it as evidence of God. Oh, I enjoyed being outside when I was little, taking my collie for a walk or having imaginary adventures in the woods behind our house. And Springtime would thrill me, with all the newborn leaves and grass after the bareness of Winter.

But I didn't know enough about God then to recognize the world as His handiwork. And it certainly didn't lead me to declare God's glory out loud. It wasn't until I started studying the Bible that I began to acknowledge the wonders just beyond my window for what they were - living expressions of God's majesty.

Now that I know better, His creative hand is evident all around me - every season captures me with it's special beauty. I imagine Him designing each tree and flower with the most delicate of touches. A casual walk in the woods can lead me to declare to others how awed I am by a God who would make all this and share it with us!

Action Point:
Do you like being out in nature? Can you find something to like about every season? Take time each week to spend outdoors, even in your back yard. Really focus on what you see around you. Take in big and small details - a blade of grass or a colorful sunset. Imagine God designing and bringing this world to life, not just for Him, but for us to enjoy as well. Write down some of your observations. Who could you share those with?

_____

_____

_____

_____

_____

Day 19
Ascribe

"Ascribe to the LORD, O mighty ones, ascribe to the LORD glory and strength. Ascribe to the LORD the glory due his name; worship the LORD in the splendor of his holiness."

Psalm 29:1-2

The Merriam Webster dictionary defines "ascribe" as "to refer" a thing or quality to "a supposed cause or author." David never had any trouble coming up with holy qualities, and was excited to name the owner of them any chance he had! In this one psalm alone, David gave an impressive list of character traits of God for which he wanted His people to lift up praise: His glory and strength, and His power. David describes these poetically in verses like 5-9:

"The voice of the LORD breaks the cedars; the LORD breaks in pieces the cedars of Lebanon. He makes Lebanon skip like a calf, Sirion like a young wild ox. The voice of the LORD strikes with flashes of lightning. The voice of the LORD shakes the desert; the LORD shakes the Desert of Kadesh. The voice of the LORD twists the oaks and strips the forests bare."

The longer David walked with his God, the more amazed he became. Writing his psalms was a way to express the delight and awe that welled up inside him. Those songs were also a way to open other peoples' eyes to God's immeasurable greatness.

Prayer Starter:
There is no end to the list of attributes God displays. Write a prayer about one or two that have personal meaning for you. Give God the credit and praise for them. Then ask Him to show you someone who needs to hear about them!

_____

_____

_____

_____

_____

Day 20
Ascribe

"Ascribe to the LORD, O families of nations, ascribe to the LORD glory and strength."

Psalm 96:7

I've been trying to keep up more with current events, both for my own information and as a tool for focusing my prayers. But within the first minute of watching a newscast or reading a newspaper, my heart starts to sink. Shootings, home invasions, corruption scandals - a daunting number of "bad news" items - give the world a dark and dangerous feel.

If I'm not careful, discouragement and fear can set in. All I see is what's wrong around me. And the evil that people are capable of doing takes on a kind of power. My prayers become smaller, more centered on my own safety and provision, and and I miss the opportunity to intercede. One of the best ways I've found to counteract those negative thoughts and feelings is to look out my window. Seeing even just a glimpse of nature reminds me there is still beauty to be found, and leads me to give credit to the One who created it.

Concentrating on God keeps me in a place of worship. As I ascribe glory to God for who He is, I feel a lifting of the heaviness that the world's sin sets on me. Then I see Him at work in the lives of people more clearly, and am reassured of His ultimate victory. I am strengthened to pray for those "bad news" items with hope and determination.

Action Point:

Next time you watch the news, notice your reaction to the onslaught of negative stories. If you start to feel down or afraid, stop and write those feelings down. Then do something that reminds you of God: reading scripture, listening to worship music, stepping outside, etc. Next to each negative item, write a positive characteristic God possesses. Give God the credit for the victory in your heart and the world!

_____

_____

_____

_____

_____

_____

Day 21
Come Before Him
(Bring An Offering)

"Because of your temple at Jerusalem kings will bring you gifts."
Psalm 68:29

David loved using word pictures. Here he presents the image of God as the ultimate warrior. David starts right in with a call in verse 1 - "May God arise..." Verse 7 talks about how God "marched out" before His people, scattering and crushing the heads of their enemies. Then, in verse 24, David shares what could almost be called a vision of God's triumphant procession into His sanctuary, complete with singers and musicians, as well as the princes and tribes of Israel.

There in the temple the Almighty receives the praise He is due. Twice, in verse 18 and verse 29, David mentions God receiving gifts as a response from those who behold His power and glory. What kind of gifts? Gold, silver, precious oils and herbs were all used in Old Testament times to express worship to the Lord. But David knew the thing that would truly please Him, and stated it plainly in Psalm 51:16-17.

"You do not delight in sacrifice, or I would bring it; you do not take pleasure in burnt offerings. The sacrifices of God are a broken spirit; a broken and contrite heart, O God, you will not despise." God puts little stock in things received from people whose hearts are far from Him. He blesses those who give Him *themselves* first.

Prayer Starter:

You can give God all sorts of presents, but the one thing He desires most is your heart, your mind, your strength. Write a prayer confessing to Him the times you've held those treasures back and why. Repent of your independence, and declare your desire to be His, asking Him to show you how.

_____

_____

_____

_____

_____

Day 22
Come Before Him
(Tremble)

"Worship the LORD in the splendor of his holiness; tremble before him, all the earth."

Psalm 96:9

I have to admit - the idea of trembling before God used to seem outdated to me. Sure, examples I saw in the Bible inspired me. But Moses or Mary fell face-down in response to an *actual visit* from the Lord. No one I knew had experienced that, and I wasn't expecting it to happen. So I contented myself with a lower-key connection to God.

That belief started to change when I joined the music team at my new church. While I led the congregation, lyrics to certain songs began to reveal more to me about the big-ness of God. Soon, "How Great Thou Art"[3] and "God of Wonders"[4] began to fill me up with a new reverence and awe.

But my most intense episode of trembling before God came one weekday afternoon while doing laundry in my basement. There, right next to the dryer, I fell down on my knees in tears, overwhelmed by a new vision of the incredibly huge sacrifice that Jesus made to save me. I was overcome by the immeasurable size of God's love. Now I've had a peek at what Moses and Mary experienced - and I know that trembling is not at all outdated!

Action Point:

Do you have a sense of the big-ness of God? Read scriptures that talk about God's majesty and His glory, such as Joshua Chapter 6. Write down how God showed Himself in that battle. Now write some ways God has worked in a mighty way (though maybe in a smaller, quieter way than Jericho) in your life.

_____

_____

_____

_____

_____

Day 23
Be Glad

"But may all who seek you rejoice and be glad in you; may those who love your salvation always say, "The LORD be exalted!"

Psalm 40:16

Part of the power of David's psalms lies in his testimonies to God's faithfulness in his life. He shared his fears honestly, as well as his determination to reach for his Lord no matter how dire a situation looked. David was always quick to give praise for being protected, rescued and restored. He knew he was covered. And his spirit showed a sense of settled gladness for that.

But along with the wonderful examples David's songs give of God's care for him, they also impart hope that others can have the same experience. After telling of how God brought him out of trouble, David wrote, "Many will see and fear the Lord and put their trust in him." He goes on to describe those who believe in God as "blessed."

David had a great desire that others would feel the gladness he felt in his own heart. He knew that not everyone would respond - he started verse 16 with the word "but" to contrast the fate of those who follow God with those who reject Him. Even so, David continued to encourage and teach, convinced that some would be spurred on closer toward God.

Prayer Starter:

David gives us great examples of what it means to be glad in God. Write a prayer, stating what makes you glad about God. Is it His trustworthiness? Is it His protection? Ask for the strength to "settle in" with the knowledge of God's grace for you.

_____

_____

_____

_____

_____

_____

Day 24
Be Glad

"Rejoice in the LORD and be glad, you righteous; sing, all you who are upright in heart!"

Psalm 32:11

The Matthew Henry Bible Commentary[5] further defines "gladness" in this verse, saying of those who love God: "Let them be so transported with this holy joy as not to be able to contain themselves; and let them affect others with it, that they also may see that a life of communion with God is the most pleasant and comfortable life we can live in this world."

Worship that stirs passion and sparks momentary thrills has its place. But when I think of gladness, I think of a deeper kind of emotion. Some people I've known live their everyday lives with a combination of peace and joy, a calm, constant kind of excitement. It's as if they know a secret that brings them great enjoyment, no matter the circumstances. And being around them has led me to admire what they have and want to learn that secret!

Where does gladness come from? The answer is right at the beginning of verse 11 of Psalm 32 - rejoicing in the Lord. Spend time learning His Word and His works. Seek to become more aware of His presence in your life. Soak in the truth of His love and delight in you, and respond in song or prayer to Him. As we grow closer to God, that holy joy will build inside us. Others will be drawn to us more and more, wondering what we know!

Action Point:
Being glad is a mindset. It happens over a period of time, after making a habit of looking for the good in daily life. Spend time each day remembering God's character, and some of the ways He's shown Himself to you. Notice each positive feeling that springs up inside you (excitement, joy, relief, etc) and write them down. He wants you to "settle in" to gladness!

_____

_____

_____

_____

_____

Day 25
Cry Out

"I cry out to God Most High, to God, who fulfills [his purpose] for me."
Psalm 57:2

In this psalm, David said he was in "the midst of lions," forced to "dwell among ravenous beasts." Fear colored his words as he described the men who "hotly pursue" him, who "spread a net" for his feet. But when danger closed in on him, David knew where to run.

How many people shared David's trust in God's rescue? Were any of the soldiers that followed him aware of God's provision for them? King Saul certainly didn't have the faith to understand David's fighting Goliath with just a sling shot. And shutting God's grace out of his life resulted in jealousy and insecurity in the King's heart toward the young warrior.

Despite the doubt of Saul, and probably many others around him, David's belief remained strong through trouble. Crying out to an unseen God wasn't foolish and it wasn't weak. In fact, it was the opposite - reaching for God showed a strength of character that others hadn't yet developed, and a wisdom that others hadn't gained. And it always led him to worship and praise, which God richly rewarded.

Prayer Starter:
David had no trouble crying out to God. In fact, when things looked bleakest, David trusted all the more in God's provision. Write a prayer to God, confessing anything that keeps you from reaching for Him when you're in need. Ask Him to make it clear to you how much He loves you, and thank Him for that love!

_____

_____

_____

_____

_____

_____

Day 26
Cry Out

"The righteous cry out, and the LORD hears them; he delivers them from all their troubles."

Psalm 34:17

It may seem strange to think of crying out as a form of worship. For most of us, calling out for help demonstrates a flaw, as if we can't take care of ourselves. And it is something we often do only as a last resort after trying any other things we can think of first. But the smartest and most peaceful people have a different perspective.

Crying out to God can actually be a valuable expression of worship. But our hearts have to be right first. So what attitudes will lead us to reach out in a way that pleases God?

1. **Trust** - believing that God is faithful to hear our prayers and to answer them in His way and timing
2. **Obedience** - following the call in scripture to go to God first with our needs and troubles instead of trying to figure things out for ourselves
3. **Expectation** - claiming the promises God has given to provide help for us, placing our hope in Him

Our Jehovah Jirah is ready, willing and able to take care of us. If we're wise, we'll see asking for help as He does - as a humble offering of worship to a Lord that loves blessing us in every way.

Action Point:
Think about the last time you cried out to God for help or rescue. Were you embarrassed about asking? Were you afraid He wouldn't answer you? Or did you feel secure and settled? Write about your experience, then re-write Psalm 34:17 below it as a reminder of how much God wants to take care of you.

_____

_____

_____

_____

_____

_____

Day 27
Proclaim His Salvation

"Sing praises to the LORD, enthroned in Zion; proclaim among the nations what he has done."

Psalm 9:11

When David had won a victory in battle, lifting up praise to God was an automatic response for him. He celebrated God's might and the strength He gave the army to fight. He cheered at the defeat of his enemies. And he rejoiced in God's glory being clearly displayed for all to see. But though God wanted to bless the Israelite military, He had a bigger plan for His people - salvation from their sin.

David, having a heart for God, understood the ultimate mission well. He was acutely aware of his own sin, and of the state of the world around him. David often wrote about how disobedience to God affected his life, and he was passionate about changing the behavior he witnessed in others when they lived apart from God. He saw the problem, and he laid out the solution for the nation to see.

Long before Jesus Christ came, God gave David special insight into His heart. David got to see a heavenly Father who grieved for His lost children, who was willing to forgive and restore them at the moment they turned back to Him. His heart was filled with longing to bring them home. That glimpse fueled David's worship and his passion to make sure others heard the truth of God's powerful love.

Prayer Starter:

Getting a real sense of God's salvation is humbling - we don't deserve it, and we can never earn it. Yet by grace He offers it to us, no matter what we've done. Write a prayer to Him that proclaims what His gift of mercy means to you.

_____

_____

_____

_____

_____

Day 28
Proclaim His Salvation

"Sing to the LORD, praise his name; proclaim his salvation day after day."

Psalm 96:2

My husband and I attended "Congress," a large Christian conference in Boston, for a few years. Every time I went I was blown away - thousands of believers all gathering to sing, sit in workshops, and generally take over the Convention Center. After two days of corporate worship and soaking in ideas I was filled to the brim. Overflowing with zeal, I was ready to proclaim God from rooftops all the way back down the Mass Pike!

It didn't take long after heading home, however, for the excitement to fade. I fell back into my usual routine of expressing passion for God on Sundays while laying low the rest of the week. Instead of being bold for Jesus in my daily life, my spiritual walk was rather lukewarm. And I felt disappointed.

Psalm 96 has been a great reminder to me that every day is important to God. He gives us times, like retreats or conferences, that recharge our spiritual batteries and inspire us to worship. But He calls us to praise and proclaim Him and His works "day after day," wherever we are. Our whole lives are meant to be a testimony, not just high points. We can proclaim our Lord in quiet ways, to one person at a time, and grow God's kingdom.

Action Point:
We can do things each day to proclaim God to others. It can be directly through what we say, or indirectly through things we do. What we may think of as a small gesture can have big impact for God on someone's heart. Write down some creative ideas of what you can do to proclaim God to the world "day after day."

_____

_____

_____

_____

_____

_____

Day 29
Call on His Name

"To you I call, O LORD my Rock; do not turn a deaf ear to me. For if you remain silent, I will be like those who have gone down to the pit."

Psalm 28:1

This verse is a clear plea from David for God to respond to a need. And in verse 3 he added, "Do not drag me away with the wicked." Was David unsure of God's willingness to hear and help him? Or was he questioning how God thought of him? No - David knew God's heart well enough not to doubt His character or His judgment.

David was acknowledging his own weakness here. He wisely understood that he could not handle life alone, and that if God wasn't with him, he was sunk! In this case, David wanted protection from his enemies, and from discouragement at seeing the wicked prosper around him. God's touch could bring the relief and hope he was desperate for.

This awareness of his need wasn't reserved for times of trouble, though. It guided David through every day, whatever the circumstances may have been. He continually meditated on who God was and how He wanted to care for His people. Calling out to God had become a natural part of life for him, and another way to give his Lord the glory He deserved.

Prayer Starter:

David had a desperate desire to hear from God. He felt utterly lost without the Lord's leading in his life. Do you feel that kind of desperation for God? Write a prayer that expresses how much you want to hear from Him, and any difficulties or frustrations you have about that. Thank God for knowing your heart, and that He is so near.

_____

_____

_____

_____

_____

_____

Day 30
Call on His Name

"Will evildoers never learn-- those who devour my people as men eat bread and who do not call on the LORD?"

Psalm 14:4

This psalm is a powerful reminder to me of what I could have been like if God hadn't grabbed me out of the world. In fact, the first line states it clearly - "The fool says in his heart there is no God." And I was quite a fool for many years.

I always had a sense, even as a young child, that there was some higher power in charge. But when given opportunities as I grew to give a name to that higher power, I didn't. I rejected His Lordship in my life and ignored His commands. As a result, by the time I was 29, I felt old, like my life was "corrupted" and not what it should have been. I was "overwhelmed with dread" all the time - such an awful way to live.

Who knows what would have happened to me if I hadn't turned toward God? I see some of the ways people use and abuse others, and think "There but for the grace of God go I." Could my heart have grown so hard that I would have dismissed God's existence entirely? Or, instead of continuing to show me mercy, might He have finally given me over to my own desires? Would I have ended up an evildoer without hope of being saved? That thought scares me like no other, and leads me to call on my Heavenly Father all the more!

Action Point:

Think back on your own journey of faith. Did you always believe in God, or did you go through a time when He wasn't even a part of your life?

What about now - do you call on God's name as the one who is your all-in-all, or do you still have doubts about His ability? Do you desire His will above your own?

Imagine God writing you a letter about your walk with Him so far. Write down what you think He would want you to know about His feelings for you, and how He wants to work in your life now and going forward.

_____

_____

_____

_____

_____

NOTES

[1] Peterson, Eugene H. The Message: The Bible in Contemporary Language. Colorado Springs: NavPress, 2002. Print.

[2] Strong, James. Strong's Exhaustive Concordance: With Greek and Hebrew Dictionary. Nashville: Manna Publishers, n.d.. Print.

[3] Hine, Stuart K. How Great Thou Art. Hollywood, CA: Manna Music, 1955. Musical score.

[4] Byrd, Mark & Hindalong, Steve. God of Wonders. Brentwood, TN: EMI Christian Music Group, 2000. Musical score.

[5] Henry, Matthew. Matthew Henry's Concise Commentary on the Whole Bible. Nashville: T. Nelson, 1997. Print.

CPSIA information can be obtained
at www.ICGtesting.com
Printed in the USA
BVHW040208030520
579086BV00016B/3099